SPARE ROOM

HAIBUN VARIATIONS

SPARE ROOM

HAIBUN VARIATIONS

jim natal

poetry

TEBOT BACH • HUNTINGTON BEACH • CALIFORNIA • 2019

Cover painting: "Cambridge Bedroom" by Olivia Eielson,
    www.oliviaeielson.net
Book and cover design & author photo: Tania Baban
Cover photograph: gyro, iStock by Getty Images.

ISBN: 978-193967849-2
Library of Congress Control Number: 2019901642
A Tebot Bach book.

Tebot Bach, Welsh for little teapot, is a Nonprofit Public Benefit
Corporation, which sponsors workshops, forums, lectures, and
publications. Tebot Bach books are distributed by Small Press
Distribution, Armadillo, and Ingram.

The Tebot Bach Mission: Advancing literacy, strengthening
community, and transforming life experiences with the power
of poetry through readings, workshops, and publications.

This book is made possible by a generous donation from
Steven R. and Lera B. Smith.

www.tebotbach.org

For Tania
Without
Variation

TABLE OF CONTENTS

I have always known that one day
I would take this path though yesterday
I did not know it would be today.

—Ariwara no Narihari
(Japan, 825-880)

Westbound on Interstate 10, crossing the Colorado River on the way to L.A., 107 degrees at 11:00 a.m. On the radio Randy Newman sings about traveling the other direction— he's "going to Arizona, just a rider in the rain." He must be coming from Portland because from the looks of the Mojave in the middle of August it hasn't rained here since there were warm shallow seas. A sign on the south side of the freeway proclaims: "Food Grows Where Water Flows" as if it's a debatable concept. But if you need confirmation just ask the farmers far downstream in Mexico, where the river thins to a trickle. Or, closer to home, ask the growers and ranchers in Colorado and New Mexico, or anywhere new developments and agribusiness are elbowing aside family fields, pastures, and orchards. In those places, they have close working knowledge of agricultural physics: water, they say, runs uphill toward money.

Poor brown coyote
Slinks away thirsty again
Nothing left but salt

How fitting the total lunar eclipse would be an October blood moon. War, disease, and zealous ignorance cast shadows over the habited globe as the earth flashes a full frontal across its cratered sibling. At least the darkness on the moon passed quickly. It doesn't appear the earth will be so lucky. Gnawing at borders, straining at containment, chain reactions of brutality seem unstoppable in what's left of my lifetime. I fear for my daughter. I fear for my wife. I fear for my friends. I fear for all those of like minds and those with whom I disagree. I fear for surviving species and landscapes, for every monument of human construction or natural. I fear for history. I fear for the future. And I fear for the moon, for the inevitable war over who owns it.

Mouse and shrew cower
As raptor shade glides over
Wait for it to pass

Comet fears that vaporize near the sun. Y2K angst. Nostradamus. The Mayan Calendar Countdown, Armageddon on the Temple Mount. Then radio evangelist Harold Camping prophesied The Rapture and End Times with absolute certainty…for the third time. And now I read that Heimdallr has already blown his *Gjallerhorn* and that *Ragnarök* is at hand. Yet another Twilight of the Gods. Is the world so out of control, the future so dire—climate collapse, polarity reversal, an entire digitized world system that can go out like a night light when power massively fails; those pathetic final shallow sips of fossil fuels and untainted water. Does humanity in its heart of hearts yearn for extinction? Do we somehow know without knowing that we've reached our expiration date? Ancient Alien Theorists and the Hopi say it's happened many times before. Why would I quibble that a fresh start isn't in order? Would things turn out differently? If not, why bother beginning again? Just roll over and be done with it. By the way, credit where it's due: Camping died just weeks after his third-strike deadline passed. So, in a way, he was right about the end of life on earth.

Beauty in descent
Fall leaves float not plummet
Let go or be dragged

My wife and I talk on Skype; her night, my morning. She's visiting her mother far away who's not doing well. So difficult to steal time for us to be together, intimacy reserved for the iDevices. Postponed vacations, obligations, the to-do list that abhors a vacuum, pressing *shoulds* of family and work, even the cat more needy than ever. The computerization that made our video chat possible, that decades ago promised more leisure, just brought on more unemployment, the all-consuming Internet, the overwhelming urgency of texts, emails and tweets, an inescapable cartel of tech giants. Life in The Cloud: you can't get off it without falling farther than Icarus. I don't know about you, but we're having to schedule simple drinks and dinners with friends three months out, and then iffy and in pencil. People always tired, stressed, unwilling to commit, to drive any distance in all-hours traffic, spontaneity fast becoming a vague concept. It's slipping away, dropping off like ice cliffs in Greenland, raising the level of the sea that surely will drown us.

Shared cup of green tea
Rarer than a rainy day
In a spring of drought

After Paris in December I walked the beach. Los Angeles never looked so Gauguin, the city of sunshine versus the City of Light so "old and cold and settled in its ways." The high clouds had been washed with white ink on blue, fat *sumi-e* brush strokes dispersing as they tailed off to the East, toward the mountains and then the desert. The tide receded, revealing a boulevard of wet sand that mirrored the sky and made walking an act of levitation. It was late afternoon.
A few people had begun to gather, staking out their spaces to watch the setting of the winter sun. Almost all were alone and had settled equidistant from each other exactly like the gulls standing at the surf line facing out to sea. In a moment of shared reflection, even the ocean withdraws far into itself.

No clump of seaweed—
Long neck twisted, wings, web feet
The dead cormorant

Asian fishing bird
Trussed in filament, hooks set
An exquisite corpse

When this brutal winter is finally over, will people be fleeing the frigid East in droves and moving to southern California? After the big Northridge quake in 1994 the exodus flowed the other way—kind of like ball bearings on a titling board or amoebas responding to negative stimuli. As for me, I couldn't agree more with the song "I Love L.A." I thrive on smog, wildfires, mudslides, drive-bys, drought, raging density, constant parking hassles, interminable traffic, and police helicopters in the middle of the night. But wait, there's more! I just read in the local paper that leopard sharks have taken up residence in the Venice canals. The article assures that they "aren't dangerous to humans" even though they can grow to five feet long. Uh, huh. Like my friend said when someone on a walk asked her if her dog bites: "Well, he has teeth."

Unprecedented
Whole countries drained of people
Drowning on dry land

And now they say the cure is five years away—the same
five years the doctors predicted when I was diagnosed
more than 40 years ago. Nobody in my family loses weight
without trying. I could eat *anything*! Cookies. Brownies.
Those boxes of ice cream sandwiches from the 7-11 freezer.
And Hostess pocket fruit pies I sigh remembering. The
pounds just kept peeling off like bark. Maybe because I was
a runner then my mileage kept the hell hound at bay better
than my denial. Unquenchable thirst. Undammable stream
of urine. In another era, another country, I'd already be
dead, like my grammar school friend's mother, ghostly in
a darkened room filling a glass syringe. Needles, pumps,
and tubes. Complications. Amputation. Nerve damage.
Blindness. Counting cards in five-year increments;
like the house in Vegas, diabetes always wins.

Rising and falling
The sap in autumn maples
Blood sugar levels

Researchers report that buying doesn't make for happiness. The thrill of a new purchase wears off in about a year—if not before. But the problem isn't acquisition, it's getting rid of accumulated possessions. Anyone who's ever moved to a smaller space or dealt with disbursing the belongings of the dead has learned this the hard way. "Vintage" and "collectible" are relative terms; value is subjective. Even the thrift stores are getting picky.

My father's trophies
No shelf room now that he's gone
Flowers in landfill

Hoarder alert: business is booming in the sub-industry of storage lockers. People pile stuff in their units, pay for it years on end at a cost exponentially higher than declining material value, then walk away with the lock still on the door. My friend, who's lived in California for decades, has had a storage locker in Vermont since he left the East. Besides the body of his ex-wife in a freezer, what could be worth all those monthly bills?

Carcass left behind
Hyenas and the vultures
Bidding at auction

Counterfeit merchandise on Internet sites has become an estimated $1 trillion business, more lucrative than the international drug trade. If the online bargain price you paid for that Gucci purse, Montblanc pen, or Tiffany & Co. silver necklace was too good to be true, it was. And speaking of Internet counterfeits, how about ersatz selling events? First came Black Friday, then Cyber Monday, which got extended into Cyber Week. Now there's Green Monday. Oh, and let's not forget Giving Tuesday, so the non-profits can get their piece of the virtual mince pie. Where did these designated days come from (as if we didn't already know). Is there some sort of consortium or oligarchy that dreams up knock-off commercial holidays? Do eBay, Amazon, Alibaba, and representatives of various global corporate and government interests—a veritable fertile crescent of greed—have a clandestine sit-down in Geneva or Dubai and blue sky more ways to jimmy people from their money in the spirit of what used to be the Holiday Season? Isn't it enough to start playing "Holly Jolly Christmas" in September?

Mantis blends with leaf
Coloration bugs can't see…
Until it's too late

The old year is on its last legs. I should have taken it out
and shot it months ago, done us both a favor. In its youth
the old year went around so fast it lapped itself, so far ahead
it was behind. But sometime in September the old year made
a rookie mistake, looked back. Time closed the distance,
caught up, tapped it on the shoulder with a heavy hand as
it passed. Now the old year gasps, sucks the oxygen out
of the room, elephants and all. My heart spurts pity and
I see the old year for the pathetic creature it has become.
Look at it— cringing by its bowl hard against the corner
of the refrigerator and tomorrow. As my father used to say,
"Isn't that a hell of a note?"

Floating spiderweb
Brushes my face in my sleep
A strand of your hair

New Year's Day. Time for a remodel, an extensive months-down-the-drain, years-down-the-drain, fill the money pit to the lip, feed the kitty 'til it pukes, fourth-and-long with-time-running-out-in-the-final-quarter *extreeeme* makeover. Redecorate. Renovate. Lose weight. Work out. Get a grip on those love handles. A one helping, small plate, half-piece-o'-pizza limit. Strictly enforced. Zero tolerance. And I repeat, zero. Call in the contractors, the landscapers, plumbers and electricians, the roofer, floor guy, tile man and painter. Suck it in and hold it up. Tone up. Tighten up. Straighten up. Shape up. Man up. Here comes the dead of winter. And you're not ready.

Strategic default
Crabs have the right idea
Molt and walk away

I've lived long enough to see the Bible proven wrong. The rich have inherited the earth. Ever seen the old black-and-white TV show *The Millionaire* in which some fictional down-and-outer was given a check for a million dollars, tax free, by philanthropist Michael Anthony? Chump change. Speaking of television, *The Six Million Dollar Man* from the 1970s is being re-booted as, what else, *The Six Billion Dollar Man*. In other words, worth is measured in billions now. When was the last time you heard about a corporate merger, a start-up buyout, with a figure in the millions? Any CEO mogul, hedge fund manager, ruthless dictator, international criminal, App creator, or Super PAC mega-donor worth his pink sea salt has nine zeros in his Panamanian/Cayman (previously Swiss) bank account. Of course, life is not all roses and cherry bowls for billionaires. It's as hard to park all that cash (legit or not) as it is to find an unpermitted space on a Santa Monica side street. Now that bank laundries are under close scrutiny, I hear Miami high-rise condos are being bought and gambled like casino chips. Shrewd move…until sea levels rise and those investments are deeper underwater than a middle-class mortgage.

Elephants, blue whales,
Himalayan mountain peaks
Too big to fail

Everything's a "brand." The term no longer is reserved for companies or organizations; people are brands, your likeness/body/mind as a commodity, a product to be differentiated from others, like Tide detergent from All, or the dozen variations of dish soap that all look to be the same. Without personal brands how could we tell the teenage influencers all over YouTube apart? Life is capitalism, the "corpus" in corporation, and the rules of the marketplace apply. Your brand can be famous simply for being famous as long as you're trending well or have a celebrated booty. Bad behavior doesn't necessarily kill your career or credibility, but it does damage your brand, even as it increases brand awareness. Get caught with a prostitute or mistress, brag about grabbing a pussy, coldcock your girlfriend in an elevator video; if you're a sports or movie star your brand can make a comeback—you could even be elected president. Anyone else's brand goes down in flames, disappears off the screen faster than Anthony Weiners's wiener. You lose your value to other brands as the sponsors and entourage go screaming for the exits. The brand stink is on you like seared steerhide as the red-hot iron presses in. Quit bitching about income inequality. It's brand eat brand out there.

Chum draws circling sharks
Scavengers swallow what's left
Big fish, bigger fish

If patriotism is the last refuge of a scoundrel, the Great
American Songbook is the last refuge of aging rock stars.
And why not? These are the songs they grew up hearing,
songs that played on their parents' phonographs outside
closed bedroom doors, that got their parents dancing in
ballrooms and through the Second World War. Bob Dylan
croons Irvin Berlin, Willie Nelson smokes some "Stardust,"
Rod Stewart cranks five albums thanks to George and Ira.
Pretty soon Springsteen and Patty Scialfa will whirl like
Fred and Ginger to a Cole Porter tune instead of leaping
off amplifiers. Why should Billie Holiday and Sarah
Vaughn be the only ones with the keys to the treasury?
The vault is open and, hey Keith Richards, put the
"hammer" back in Hammerstein. Just swagger in.

Rufous hummingbird
Hovering at its flower:
Prelude to a Kiss

Levity is in dangerously short supply—unless you count the Internet deluge of cute cat videos. Laughter's aquifer level has been dropping lower by the month—Joan Rivers, Robin Williams, Bernie Mac, Phyllis Diller, Sid Caesar, Jonathan Winters, now Gary Shandling and Don Rickles have taken final bows. On television, I mostly hear gallows humor with punch lines like a shot to the solar plexus. Monsanto is corralling the world's food supply with GMO seeds; that's why they call their carcinogenic weed killer Round-Up. (Yee hah!). Job growth is on the rise…because so many families need three of them to survive *[insert canned laugh track here]*. Hey, take our Senators and Congressional Representatives (please!). I remember a saying in *Zap Comix* from back in the hippie Haight heyday: "Dope will get you through times of no money better than money will get you through times of no dope." Well, humor will get you through times of Outrage, Fear, and Despair better than Outrage, Fear, and Despair will get you through times of no humor. And, this is—wait for it—no joke.

Those guffawing gulls
Atop that dockside streetlamp
Better wear a hat

You can get by with English almost anywhere these days,
which, in my case, is a good thing. Consider my French.
I thought I heard him say *bateau Parisien* (Parisian boat).
Or was it *gâteau Parisien* (Parisian cake)? Actually, what he
said was that he was surrounded by *affreux Parisiens* (dreadful
Parisians). Who am I to disagree? But it's no longer necessary
to travel to test one's language skills. The other day in a mobbed
L.A. market my wife and I may have been the only ones
speaking English. Blindfolded, what country were we in?
Your globalized guess is as *bon, bueno,* or *jayyid* as mine.

Wind shimmies the palms
Right out of their frilly fronds
Spring's rough translation

This is a measure of how cynical I've become. I see a commercial for a credit monitoring service and immediately think they're paying hackers to steal identities so that they can create more victims and, thus, more business. Kind of like a home security firm hiring ex-con burglars to break into houses. On the subject of nefarious break-ins, is there any computer system that can't be hacked? Just ask Sony, Target, JPMorgan, or...the Houston Astros. Even U.S government agencies aren't invulnerable to electronic incursions from China, Russia, or (dare I say it) North Korea. Oh, and then there are our elections. When you've got an untraceable server, an iris or fingerprint transplant isn't necessary. Some corrupt official in Guangzhou could be driving a Mercedes purchased with funds swiped from Dubuque school pensions. But there's no going back, is there? It's hard to hide money under a Sleep Number bed. Personally, I think it's all Ben Franklin's fault; he should have known better than to fly a kite in a storm.

She searches the beach
For a perfect sand dollar
Holes pecked in each one

Wild symbiosis
Moth and yucca, mistletoe
Friends with benefits

Has AIDS been cured? I don't think so. But you'd never know it from reading *Cosmo* or about Millennial hook-ups and "sugar dates" on Tinder, OkCupid, Happn, and SeekingArangements. iSex is as casual as a phone swipe with no future expectations or commitments from any gender. I thought that's what hookers were for. "Tinderellas" obviously think otherwise. And who can single them out? Sex is ubiquitous; every magazine ad, billboard, movie, and sitcom *double entendre* is fraught with references and content. Don't get me wrong. I took full advantage of the "Free Love" of my hippie days. But at least you had to work at it a bit, deploy a dependable pick-up line beyond a texted "Wanna fuck?" or at least have a full baggie *sans* stems and seeds. The current coupling process is so damn quick and easy—the electronic version of consensual in this #metoo moment. I'm mature enough to know sex rarely is free no matter who it's with. Am I just envious that dating apps didn't exist when I was younger and that my "Dad bod" precludes poaching them now? Maybe a little…Maybe more.

Black widow spiders—
Watched them mate but didn't tell him
Why ruin pleasure?

My cat Dante has recently taken to sleeping on the pillow behind my head. It reminds me of the coonskin cap I wore as a kid in mid-50's Chicago. I was crazy for *Davy, Davy Crockett, King of the Wild Frontier.* My favorite t-shirt of all time was yellow and had scenes from Davy's exploits: Indian Fighter, River Pirates, Congressional Pirates, and the Alamo, where he died with Colonel Travis and Jim Bowie, famous for the knife that still carries his name. Speaking of names, I used to pretend I was named for Jim Bowie instead of great grandfather Judah on my father's side. Even now I think a man needs a good blade, albeit not necessarily a foot-long "Arkansas Toothpick." And Fess Parker, the rangy actor who played my hero *who kilt him a bear when he was only three*, went on to make himself, like Davy, *a legend forevermore*—except he parlayed his screen legend into pricey Santa Barbara resorts and wineries. I never imagined back then I'd be *followin' Davy into the West*, and that nearly seven decades later I'd be sitting in Parker's hotel lobby sipping his signature Syrah, pretending, again like Davy, *I'm the man who don't know fear.*

Human arrogance
Brings knives to nature's gunfight
Inadequate edge

Another action film leaves me shaking my head. How can so many guys in tactical black be such bad shots? When world-threatening super villains are staffing up their organizations, do they interview prospective recruits at the gun range and only hire the ones with the biggest muscles and the worst target groupings? You know the scenes: the good guys go sprinting helter skelter across pipes, beams, and catwalks in evildoers' sprawling industrial complexes (that, of course, no one noticed being built) while hordes of uzi-toting henchmen open fire. Rounds ping off handrails, spatter walls, shatter plate glass but not one bullet in the high-caliber beeswarm, not one tiny piece of metal flake or missile shard of windshield finds its mark, not even by fluke—unlike the real-life New York City cop who killed a suspect with a single ricochet in a dark stairwell. Come on, half the senior citizens in Arizona can shoot better than these studio bozos. In movies, as in finance and politics, the bigger the budgets, the worse the aim.

Juking to stay dry
Making music in the rain
Spaces between drops

Climate change naysayers. Unproven science. Fake news. The sky is falling down in flames. The hottest year on record worldwide and the new year promises to be hotter yet. But don't sweat it. This has all happened before and we survived, didn't we? So what if Phoenix and furnace are now interchangeable terms? So what if the polar caps are melting like ice chips in a Happy Hour margarita? Oh, and ignore that 70-mile crack in the Antarctic glacier that calved like a gargantuan white cow and those year-round forest fires and hurricanes. Repeat after me and a sage Oklahoma senator, along with an actual climate scientist (who also believes smoking doesn't cause lung cancer): global warming isn't real and it's not our fault. Why make a volcano out of an anthill? Trust us—ninety-seven percent of the world's scientists *can* be wrong.

Dandelion clocks
So much for humanity
Dries up, blows away

I just received notice that next year there will be no increase in Social Security benefits. "The law," and I quote, "does not permit an increase in benefits when there is no increase in the cost of living." I don't know what fiduciary bizarro world government accountants live in but apparently it's one without supermarkets. A bag of groceries that used to cost $20 now costs upwards of $40. And I'm not talking non-GMO, hormone-free, organic items at Whole Foods, just standard foodstuffs. Granted, eggs became expensive because a disease almost laid Midwestern chicken populations to rest. But what about everything else in our sticker-shock shopping carts? Yes, there are deals to be had on apparel; Macy's has a Special-Lowest-Prices-of-the-Year-One-Day Sale just about every day. And, true, it is possible to find a decently equipped certified "pre-owned" car for less than $30,000 out the door. Speaking of cars, it sounds like the fiscal curve breaker is gasoline. The Social Security baked bean counters point to gas prices being so low as to counterbalance retirees' other expenses. Well, there you have it: Let them eat oil.

Easy to find slugs
There among the garden leaves
Those slippery tracks

Am I the only person on the planet who hasn't yet given a
TED Talk? That's not all. It used to be that having a personal
website and Facebook page were enough, an Internet catalog
of accomplishments for all the cyberworld to tweet. But even
TED Talks have been eclipsed. I'm starting to get the feeling that
in order to truly boost oneself out there beyond mere global
superstardom, one must be the subject of a documentary film.
It's possible that in the next 20 years everyone will have a digital
"reel." Instead of "Here's my card" it'll be "Watch my biopic."
Filmmakers won't even have to wait until the subjects are dead.
They already don't; someone's whole existence up to now
just fodder for a trailer. In fact, living documentaries could be
a thriving business for film school graduates who couldn't
cut it in Hollywood or Bollywood or Hong Kong—the
wedding singers of digicam. Your life in lights coming soon
to a flat screen near you.

Twenty-year-old stars
Write autobiographies
Mayflies live one day

Love those unicorns! That's the new Siliconic term for start-up companies valued at more than a billion dollars before they're barely out of the stable. As you read this, yet another 20-year-old has become a gazillionaire after tinkering on some supra-tech virtuality in his parents' garage. When I was a kid the only things in my parents' garage (besides my father's enormous Buick Electra) were 50-pound bags of rock salt for me to lug and scatter on our icy sidewalks, thus melting latent lawsuits from passersby. Last night at a birthday party I listened to a bearded young guy in a plaid flannel shirt explain what he does for a living—something about creating and embedding video in mobile devices. The concepts he described are not even in my mind-set let alone my skill set. I write with pen on yellow legal pads. My wife can set type by hand. Come see us when the power goes down. It'll only cost a few million for us to help you out.

Turtle's carapace
Keeps rain and predators out
Shell corporation

There's a reason it's called *minimum* wage. For the sake of easy math, let's say you make California's current mandated minimum of $10 an hour and you luck out and can work a 5-day, 40-hour week. And let's say that you somehow get paid for your half-hour lunch break, and your boss doesn't short your check. That means your take-home pay would be $400 a week, $1,600 a month, minus whatever stones the government can squeeze. The median apartment rent in L.A. has climbed to well over $1,500. So where does the money for food and utilities and gas or bus fare come from? Maybe you'll pick up a second job. Or a third. Or a few payday loans. And your spouse will, too. What if you get sick? What if you have kids? Who pays for child care while you're putting in your 12 to 16? And the much-trumpeted incremental increases in minimum wage to $13, then $15 an hour? They don't take full effect for years. Keep scraping by until then. This wouldn't be an issue if you were, according to an OXFAM report, among the 26 individuals on the planet whose total wealth is greater than the worth of the poorest half of the world's 3.8 billion people combined. If you can afford a phone, start making some calls. Maybe one of those 26 has a spare room.

Green socialism
Some bees gather more pollen
Still share with the hive

When I think of Switzerland I think of health. I visualize
herds of tan cows with bells roaming pristine alpine meadows
ringed by snow-capped peaks. I visualize spry octogenarians
in front of windows thrown wide open on winter mornings
doing deep breathing exercises. Well, I just returned from a trip
to Geneva and I couldn't believe how many people there still
smoke. Granted, smoking isn't permitted inside restaurants, but
non-smokers are on their own if they decide to sit outside in a
café to enjoy a *ristretto* on a sunny day. Being in the vicinity of
wafting exhaled smoke makes my lungs feel like they're crouching
in an attic room in a house fire. I have to grudgingly admit
that even the French (the French!) do a better job of shielding
non-smokers. Then there are the Japanese, who put signs up at
thronged Tokyo intersections warning smokers about holding
cigarettes at their sides while waiting to diagonally cross lest they
jab the lit end in the eye of a child. My wife used to smoke, but
I helped her quit, telling her I wouldn't kiss her if she smelled
or tasted like cigarettes. My mother smoked cigarettes most of
her life and while pregnant with me, which may explain a few
things. My dad smoked cheap cigars while performing a variety
of household tasks, such as watching football games on two TVs
simultaneously. The chewed butts could be found still lying in
ashtrays at cereal time, a shade of olive-drab brown like things
I'm too delicate to mention. But, despite the mini-rant above,
I try to be reasonable. After all, I did grow up in the 1960s and
do live in progressive California. So I understand there's smoking
and then there's (wink, wink) *smoking*.

Swirling, re-forming
Starlings high above a field
Bird kaleidoscope

It could be said that there are two kinds of people in America—those who voted for Hillary Clinton and those who voted for Donald Trump. But that would be too pat, too simplistic, and wouldn't include those disgruntled voters who supported Bernie Sanders or those who chose in various ways and for various reasons to sit that 2016 election out. It might be better to divide by those who think of Edward Snowden as a patriot or those who see him as a traitor. Or by those who think Julian Assange performs some useful public service and those who don't. Or by those who'd move to Canada in a heartbeat if it were warmer and those who will stay in this country come hell or high water, both of which have already arrived. Keen for America. Dream for America. Flee from America. *Which side are you on, boys? Which side are you on?*

The leopard wonders
How he'd look in tiger stripes
Same hunt, new disguise

"How many MacArthur grant winners and scientists in general, are God-fearing people? What do you think the average is?" This was the final question of the evening at a panel discussion with eight MacArthur "genius" grant winners—a real showstopper posed by a woman way in the back of the auditorium who announced that she was an "evangelical." The question was delicately defused by the senior member of the panel, who had received his grant for his writings about religion. Now, days after the event, I'm thinking about how pervasive God is in America. From the Boy Scout oath to "do my duty to God and my country," to "In God We Trust" on our money, to swearing in witnesses and presidents on the Christian bible and beyond, as if God is our most prominent founding father. My sisters and I were the only Jewish kids in the public grammar school we attended in northern Indiana in the late 1950s. We had to recite "The Lord's Prayer" at the start of every school day in lock-step with the hand-over-heart, "one nation under God" of the "Pledge of Allegiance." I remember the day my teacher, Mrs. Sprague, with the tight gray hair bun, steel rim glasses, and black lace-up, block heeled shoes, took me into a janitor's closet because she overheard me say "jeez" on the playground at recess. There, in the near dark, she told me she hated how "you people" took the name of "our Lord" in vain. I guess I just took her name in vain, too.

Thunderstorm, lightning
In the middle of the night
A higher power

SAFE, WARM, IF, L.A....

Event horizon
No one here gets out alive
Memory's black hole

Tall ships, two hundred years of America, palm trees and
independence shimmying in the heat. My first summer in Los Angeles,
crashed unscripted in the guest room of a couple I barely knew at the
farthest margin of Santa Monica, where a ripple from a stone thrown
into the Bay would widen to the east until it backwashed against the
breakwater of Interstate 10—a freeway not an expressway. I watched
rush hour traffic jams outside the kitchen window, cops pulling
drivers over. Every acquaintance since has branched from there like
capillaries and canyon roads, like backward brackets in a tournament
chart. L.A. was brazen that Bicentennial July, a wide and garish
necktie that didn't quite make it down to the beltline, a Zen riddle
whose only answer was "What's so funny?" if you laughed too.

Rain, snowcaps, mudslides
Then it doesn't rain for years
Fountain of sorrow

Beater '66 VW bus, New Mexico plates, every lane a slow lane with
a horizontal steering wheel and the turning radius of a tramp
freighter. Immediate pilgrimage to 77 Sunset Strip, the 1960's TV
show that had set the California hook. Except it wasn't there; no
door beside Dino's Lodge where the investigations office should
have been and the address had four numbers instead of double
lucky sevens. L.A. illusion/disillusion. Should have known things
are not necessarily what they appear to be; art and artifice, fiction
and nonfiction intertwined, sometimes interchangeable. Bedside
Raymond Chandler had it right—that saffron filtered afternoon light
turns harsh in an instant, shows all the wrinkles and scars, the bus
ticket disappointments. Wasn't that what kept the private eyes in
business? Not so apparent then that L.A. was the city the future relied
upon, a destiny cast from character actors, drugstore counters, and
reinvention. You are who you say you are until proven otherwise.

Next revolution
This old world keeps spinnin' round
The pier carousel

Mornings. Crows squawking, hummingbirds zipping, parrots in the fronds, and noisy little finches flocking like extras, promoting themselves. Even plants were Birds of Paradise. The weather always sunny side up, taking up barely three minutes of the local newscast, floral days following one after another like Rose Bowl floats. People told me they missed having seasons. All this Chicago boy cared about was that one season had gone missing, was presumed dead. I asked where all the "fruits and nuts" were, staple fodder for the L.A. jokes on the New York late night talk shows (before the hosts relocated West). "You want that?" a new friend shrugged. "Just go down to Hollywood Boulevard." Went once, no need to go back. Bought into the dream, didn't want to undream it.

Shoreline silver coins
Tide checks out but never leaves
Midnight grunion run

Academy Awards rehearsal. Exit through the artist's door, blinding sidewalk glare, dozens of cameras raised then dropped, Doppler murmur surfing through the crowd—"It's nobody…nobody…nobody." Hit me like a commuter train except there weren't any, ego pulped in a blender, wondered if I'd made a mistake, should have tried San Francisco instead, worn flowers in my hair ten years too late. Scenes and scenery more oppressive than over-whitened teeth, ostentatious displays of wealth, unaffordable, unattainable even in my gold chain screenwriter fantasies. The beautiful women in restaurants accompanied by even more beautiful men. The Porsche convertibles. Cantilevered canyon houses and Malibu infinity pools. My friend laughed, took pity, divulged the secret combination: "They don't own any of it. Everyone's in hock up to their eyeballs."

Unfettered, alive
The only faultlines are yours
Lost maps to the stars

I hear about the steel mill in Johnstown, PA—employed 11,000
in its heyday of molten pours, now reduced to a skeleton of 100.
The nearby coal mine that fueled the furnaces shut down. The air
compressor plant moved to Mexico. Residents in the local café
mourn the losses, memories fresh of what work is, their neighbors
staggered on low-wage shifts, goodbyes to the best-liked girls
who leave each year for promises and other cities. No one seems
to care as much about the toxic river that's cleaner now, or the
once permanent haze that no longer hangs in the valley sky.
Air and water, elemental as they may be, can't provide a paycheck.
Coffee drinkers at the counter don't read the parts of the paper
or watch the segments on TV news (depending on the network
viewed) that prove with actual facts that automation takes more
jobs than outsourcing ever will. Ask the tellers, supermarket
checkers, the parking lot attendants and elevator operators. Ask
at the car parts factories, and, yes, at the mill. What's gone is gone
and it isn't coming back, no matter how often or early you vote,
no matter your resolve, your president, or the muscle of your will.

No birds this autumn
A permanent migration
Good seasons then flown

The actress explains why she turned her lovely back on the "picture business" at what many considered the height of her career. How the dictatorial studio head who'd nurtured her rise had died; the scripts he used to find for her gone incognito. How the roles she once would have been offered were given to the next young thing. She could have stayed and fought for parts, she says, but didn't. Instead, she moved to the woods one state north, established a menagerie of domesticity, now married to a local for more than 30 years. She still has her considerable art skills, appears happy, says she just wants to be loved. But the mental illness, she confides, that runs through her family likely has established a tributary. Maybe that's why she was considered "difficult" when she was working. There's a difference between giving up and leaving. You already have to be *somebody* to choose to walk away. Otherwise, how would they know you're gone?

Daily zen practice
My Ryoanji garden
Raking cat litter

I am such a sucker for women musicians. Singer-songwriters, of course, but better yet, cellists, violinists, pianists, harp and sax players. Heavily inked and pierced rock stars…not so much, but I'm open. At a concert the other night I fell for a Korean *haegeum* player even though I knew nothing about her enchanting instrument. I can't tell you how many I've crushed on over the years—a symphony of fantasy females. And there are new additions to the orchestra and chorus all the time. History is awash with men being lured to their dooms by Sirens, Lorelei, little mermaids, etc. But I'm no Odysseus and don't ever consider tying myself to the mast. I just blindly float the lilting melodies and my heart (among other organs) simply follows.

Oh Lord, please save me
From lovely soulful women
Bow, pluck, plink, and strum

When I'm king—or president—whichever happens first, I'm going to fix a few things authoritarian-style. First off, rock songs will no longer be allowed to fade out. They will have to come to a proper conclusion. Everything ends, especially songs. Speaking of music, only singers born and raised in the South or Texas will be allowed to slur their words in a drawl. The same goes for airline pilots. If you're really from Connecticut—or London—you just don't sing (or talk) that way. Next will be toothpaste. If the ingredient lists of the various formulations within a brand are basically identical, they will have to be marketed with the same package label. Just make one singularly great product with all the benefits (extra whitening, breath freshening, enamel strengthening, cavity prevention, and so on) and move on. Then there are convoluted computerized customer service phone menus: they're gone. Don't tell me how important my call is to you. If it were, humans would immediately be on the other end of the line. Oh, and the next time you order checks, you'll get an adequate number of deposit slips free. Account service charges? They're gone, too; why should banks charge *you* for getting to play with your money? I'll also be having a little meeting with electronics manufacturers; it's not going to cost more to repair items than to replace them anymore. And all airline seats will be first-class size with first-class leg room; they won't recline at meal time, either. In fact, my first 100 days will be so positive, so productive that soon there won't be any reason for me and my position to exist, elected or otherwise. I'll just get quieter and quieter and quieter and quieter, singing the same refrain over and over until I'm not there at all…

It comes and goes and
Comes and goes and comes and goes
And comes and goes and

I blame it on the aliens—interstellar not illegal. Whether they were here thousands of years ago, or they walk among us now in whatever guises, or they *are* us from some parallel/future dimension, it's obviously their fault. They could have changed this with the tiniest tweaks to our DNA, or better public instruction in ethics or conduct back when they were teaching astronomy, mathematics, and pyramid building. It's not like moving tons and tons of quarried stone blocks. It would have taken just a laser zap to a chromosome or two and we'd be living in peace and harmony—global brothers and sisters instead of constantly reconstructing contentious Babels across the planet. Or how about a public appearance coupled with a warning as in *The Day the Earth Stood Still*—you know, get it together or else. But no. The extraterrestrials just take their sky box seats and let the games begin. Good luck to all the competitors. My mother always used to say she didn't interfere. But she did. And now here I am pleading for some other-worldly parental interference and we get only radio telescope silence. I may as well be trying to contact her.

Walls without mortar
Stone circles around the globe
Secrets but no bones

I'm taking up chess. At least that's what I fantasize for a nanosecond. Then I think, why bother? Even international grandmasters get checkmated by an algorithm in record time. The rush to Artificial Intelligence is way past frightening. Software engineers and their neural scientist accomplices are brilliant people. Forget the road to hell, they're on the freeway to making themselves at best inconsequential or, more probable, obsolete with the rest of us along for the brief ride. The next step is computers with mobility and dexterity, augmenting human anatomy with biomechanical parts, or dispensing with biology altogether, replicating something more durable than organs and flesh. And then comes computers generating their own incomprehensible language, as in the hushed-up experiment where the plug had to be pulled. How many HAL 9000s, *Bladerunners*, and *Minority Reports* does it take to actuate the disturbing premises—the unstoppable inexorable inevitable? Hey, wait a minute: aren't all those dystopian screen visions generated by computer? Who's programming who?

So used to nature
Moving at a glacial pace
Until the melting

Just because you can do something doesn't mean you should.
Are you listening AI researchers, DNA splicers, gene CRISPRs,
nerve agent chemists, space-based laser death ray developers,
sonic wave weapon deployers, DARPA beetle designers,
hypersonic missile technicians, dolphin brainwashers,
pathogen biochemists, 5G kill switchers, face-recognition
coders, and particle beam engineers? I didn't think so.
And don't get me started on clones, killer robots, cyborgs,
androids, and autonomous drones…

Too full from the kill
Wolf pack lets caribou pass
Enough is enough

I'm not much of a gambler. The glitz of Vegas is lost on me.
Unless you're *Casino Royale* caliber, I just don't see the point,
the boozy appeal of the "Rat Pack." Unlike my late friend
Gerald who used to route his road trips to hit as many Indian
casinos as possible. Or my friend Carla, who, I must admit, is
pretty lucky and supplements household income with a few
hours a week working the slots. Maybe it's genetic—my father
was a terrible card player. The first gift I ever remember buying
him was a book titled, *How to Win at Poker.* Didn't help.
I think with three daughters and a strong-willed wife he
relished an excuse to be out with the guys, sit around a table,
drink Miller High Life and smoke cigars. He was willing to
pay for that by losing. You wanna play a real game of chance?
Stand in a crowded marketplace in Baghdad or Kabul,
or a ration line on a side street of what once was Aleppo.
Or you could always attend a concert in Paris…

Quick nervous glances
Dry season watering hole
Calculated risk

When it comes to world religions and comedy, Jews are in a proverbial league of their own. They've been killin' it for ages. Not many jokes begin "A priest, a rabbi, and an imam walk into a bar." To my knowledge, there's no Borscht Belt-style proving ground for comics in upstate Saudi Arabia and I sincerely doubt there's open mic night at the Vatican. Then there's fundamentalist groups like The Taliban, Isis, Boko Haram, and Al-Qaeda, all not known for their senses of humor. It's hard for audiences to chuckle if they've been decapitated. A huge percentage of comedians, now and past, are Jewish. Maybe it's because Jewish kids had to learn to keep the bullies at bay with quips instead of fists; if they're amused they probably won't punch you and get their hands all cut up on your braces. Not that there aren't tough Jews. Where I grew up on the sout' side of Chicago there were some Jewish guys you wouldn't want to mess with. And don't forget Meyer and Bugsy. (PC police please note: I said "tough" not "exemplary.") Given the history of the Jews and all they've endured—pharaohs, inquisitions, Russian pogroms, Nazi camps, the current rash of semi-automatic hate crimes— if Jews couldn't laugh how could they go on? Perhaps there's a direct correlation between surviving oppression and comedy. That's why some of the best stand-ups currently are black.

Full moon and two cats
Squalling, backs arched, tails puffed up
Fighting or mating?

Beyond belief! That was my old boss's favorite expression. It's come to mind lately on a regular basis as I get barraged by *New York Times* "Breaking News" alerts or lie awake in the middle of the night listening to the latest human outrages on BBC. Beyond belief are the constant mass shootings, school lockdowns, acid attacks, military rapes, honor killings, and mass graves dug in the name of a Prophet who would be appalled by them. It's beyond belief, beyond all rational comprehension, that there are those who would deface, ransack, and destroy for all eternity antiquities and ancient sites: Palmyra, Ur, the Bamiyan Buddhas, the Baghdad museum. Beyond belief, too, are the sheer numbers of women and children sold daily into sexual slavery. But it is *beyond* beyond belief, beyond the subbasement floor of repugnance beneath which I naively assumed it impossible to descend, to hear this morning that in Beirut there is a thriving business in the trafficking of the organs of refugees fleeing Syria and other interminable conflicts who have nothing left to sell to survive but palpitating parts of themselves. It is beyond the basest boundaries of shame, beyond the established despicable extremes to which some will go in pursuit of hard currency or bitcoin. Lower than slime mold comes to mind, although that does slime mold a great disservice.

Water connects us
Carbon-based, oxygen frail
Music decomposed

El Al just lost a court case. The Israeli airline can no longer ask women to change seats if the ultra-Orthodox Jewish passenger sitting next to them objects to their proximity. The men are afraid of touching a woman other than their wives in case the extra-marital contact leads to fatal attraction. This is known as *"negiah"* in Jewish law. It turns out the woman who sued over the forced seat swap policy was a Holocaust survivor and had to be well past a certain age. What do El Al and these fervent men think is going to happen in the confines of an airplane row? It's one thing if a couple of newlyweds start going at it under a blue blanket on their way to a Hawaiian honeymoon. But two complete strangers traveling from Newark to Tel Aviv? Come to think of it, there are a lot of similarities between Orthodox Jews and fundamentalist Muslims in terms of the separation, wrapping, and restriction of women. I remember the Middle Eastern couple I saw on a street in Geneva one afternoon. He wore an expensive designer track suit open at the neck, numerous gold chains glimmering, as he sauntered, cocky, a pace or two ahead of (I assumed) his wife. She was shrouded from head to toe; even so, I sensed she was beautiful under all that fabric. Look, I know some women choose to wear the veil and I try to respect everyone's religious beliefs. It wasn't worth an international incident to deck that smug schmuck as we passed. Though, I'll admit, the thought did cross my mind.

Adapt and adopt
The way things work in the wild
"A glimpse of stocking"

Istanbul. After all the centuries it remains the crossroads. Illuminated suspension bridges link the West and silken Asia, invisible ancient bridges span to Greece and what's left of Syria. And now there's a river tunnel and renovated fortifications gone public as parks. Trophy mansions and nightclubs line teeming Bosphorus shores, modern-day sultan's palaces with plate glass picture windows. Charcoal grilled fish sold the old way from boats in the looming shadows of leviathan cruise ships. Hagia Sophia designated a museum so foreign travelers can be astounded without removing their shoes. The Pera Palace bar still serves cocktails, pots of tea, and fleeting glimpses of Agatha Christie's ghost. *Simit* vendors pervade every street and luscious gooey *dondurma* stalls scoop impossible flavors, savory and sweet. On Istiklal Caddesi high heels navigate cobblestones and trolley tracks, click by branded Eurostyle shops—Adidas, Benetton, Zara—standing in solidarity with ubiquitous Apple and Gap. This could be any U.S. mall. But it's not.

Riot police mass
Near historic Taksim Square
Ambulances wait

Istanbul. There's no escape from amplified calls to prayer grating from ancient speakers. To some it's fundamental as air, a reassuringly regular religious clock; others hear shrill sirens, ominous overtures, off-key supplication in desperate tones. People we meet confide they're frightened. They don't know which way the government will tip: Europe or the Middle Ages. *Abayat* and *niqab* grow abundant in the spice markets, at tram stops, on sidewalks climbing the punishing hills to Galata Tower. Suicide bombs and a dubious coup. Prisons fill with journalists and teachers. Meanwhile, *madrasas* sprout on the edge of the city where boys in Nike t-shirts, girls in white *hijabs*, recite *Quran* by heart. In the coffee shop outside the Grand Bazaar, burley males smoke *sheesha*, glower at tourists through the aromatic haze, keep checking for messages on their phones.

Chewing tender leaves
Green caterpillars and snails
Garden holy war

Fourth of July. Fireworks going off all over the neighborhood well into the early morning hours. Instead of thinking about independence and the astonishingly brave Broadway-worthy founders of our country, all I can think of is the civilians trapped in Syria and other war-ravaged lands who try to sleep through deadly, not festive, explosions, the nonstop cherry bomb chatter of small arms fire and automatic weaponry, tracers and flares, not sparklers, lighting up the atmosphere. I can push the ear buds deeper and turn up the volume to mask the noise. How would it feel, I wonder, to lay in your concrete hiding space knowing that any second a jet could thunder low and destroy what's left of your family, what's left of the building where you've been surviving? Or do you sit up exhausted in the dark at a table (if you have one) drinking tea (if you have some) in a room (that isn't yet rubble) resigned to the missile or sniper's bullet with your name on it? When in the course of human events it's come to this...

Some burst like asters
Chysanthemums, peonies
The night-blooming sky

The new pharaohs' curse
May you live in a time of
Disasters and change

Fire and water. The national news smolders and flows this
morning and I'm not talking politics. These are elemental
problems beyond contentious legislators. Arizona burns from
the Mexican border to the high desert while California braces
for the consequences of the reversal of its drought fortunes—
potential flooding and infrastructure damage caused by
accelerated snowmelt runoff. This is what happens when
a double Sierra snowpack meets record heat. And speaking of
record heat, who knew certain commercial planes can't fly
when the temperature hits 120 degrees? Meanwhile, on
a Republican planet far, far away, experts who are supposed
to be on alert for dire climate scenarios are being stifled or
fired (no pun intended). And as for the rest of us here in
the Southwest? If we're not dealing with cracked dams and
"roofalanches," it'll be more wildfires. I guess we should
wrap ourselves in blankets, drop to the ground, and roll.

No show tunes involved
That smoke on the horizon
The hills are alive

An overflowing swamp. A treacherous, treasonous president.
A ventriloquist dummy vice-president. A corrupt cabinet gorging
at a self-serve buffet, Russian caviar as an appetizer, sour cream
and collusion on the side. A particularly loathsome majority
leader skipping hand-in-hand with invertebrate senatorial
sultans of smarm down a red brimstone highway to an Oz
the evangelicals can't even imagine. And thirty percent of the
population comprised of dog whistle intransigents. Meanwhile,
in Japan, the Metropolitan Intercity Railway Company issues a
public apology for any inconvenience caused by a train that left
Minami-Nagareyama station twenty seconds too early. So many
possible connections missed. So much wringing of white-gloved
hands, as other hands across the sea are grasping, grabbing,
fishy cold, short-fingered, and filthy, daring to be pried from their
ARs and bump-stocks. It's unconscionable. Devastational. Resist.

Sky is threatening
Forecast of November storms
Look the other way

Make them rich. That's the screenwriter's secret. If your characters are wealthy, beautiful, and powerful you can dispense with plot elements like scraping, scratching, and scrounging to pay bills and taxes, feed the family—you know, all the things most people have to do. The dynasties in the scripts can then get on with their illicit sex, power grabs, schemes, deals and wheels that so fascinate us 99-percenters. The other night I watched a documentary made by a famous comedy writer ostensibly about peak living after ninety. The film mostly focused on a group of his equally famous and talented nonagenarian show biz cronies. It was good to see those icons still so lucid, funny, and productive at their advanced ages. Almost everyone in the film was comfortable, had money—big money, big houses in southern California with mailboxes full of residual checks. One of the principals could no longer drive so he had a personal driver for his luxe car. Another indulged his wife a third his age with a private recording session backed by major studio sidemen who used to play with Sinatra. Yes, those featured geezers had suffered personal losses like anyone living that long, and they had earned their prosperity with their wits; they weren't born with trust funds. But I couldn't help wondering about men with a lifetime behind them of laying bricks, fixing pipes, or working a machine, or a single grandmother cleaning houses and raising her daughter's kids, or a checker with back-to-back shifts at Wal-Mart then Target trying to stay afloat: where's the film about them?

Going through garbage,
Rotten tomatoes, sour grapes
Raven makes a meal

The literary world is having what they call in the financial world a "correction." If you're not under 30, female or an alternate or indeterminate gender with lots of letters in your self-identification, if you're not of color with an exotic mixed ethnic background writing under an even more exotic-sounding (to Americans) name, you don't stand much of a chance nowadays no matter how unique or creative your writing. Publication envy? Nah, simply a statement of fact, the way things are. Old white guy poets and authors had it locked-up for decades. They were the arbiters, fired the canon from their Manhattan towers, Ivy League campus offices, and only gave non-East Coast non-conformers—beyond the mostly Caucasian beat poets—a shot on alternate leap years between 11:47 p.m. and midnight. Oh well, "The old road is rapidly age-in'," as Dylan sang so many decades ago when it was our turn to re-make the world. "Please get out of the new one if you can't lend your hand." Go look it up.

Like shale or peat bog
Layer upon dead layer
Fossil manuscript

Back when I was a kid and World War II was over but still moribund and movies of courageous American soldiers were on TV in black-and-white and Chicago stations signed off at midnight with grainy images of military air power, sea power, artillery while the national anthem played, the flag waved and my comic books featured grizzled GI superheroes growling jut-jawed about "Krauts" and "Jerrys" and Julius and Ethel Rosenberg got the chair for being Soviet spies and I heard my parents talking about our upstairs neighbors who had to flee from Austria and the DMZ divided Korea into communist north and ally south and *The Manchurian Candidate* put insidious fear of what could happen into us all and we did duck-and-cover drills at our desks at school so we could survive an atomic bomb and the HUAC hearings intimidated, ruined, tried to root out communist actors, writers, directors who had allegedly infiltrated Hollywood and walls were going up in Berlin block by block and nuclear annihilation and the communists were a stone's skip away from Miami and a game of communist dominoes was playing out in Southeast Asia while riots and protests filled the streets of home with rage, tear gas, broken glass, and fires and my father and I argued until the last rescue helicopter lifted from a Saigon rooftop and the communists had won and missiles were stockpiled, stockpiled, and counted on charts…back then the anxiety was communists under every bed, never *in* bed with our president.

Late autumn my dad
Swapping storm windows for screens
So snow won't seep in

I like monkeys as much as the next guy. But there's one species of monkey that needs to be erased from the face of the earth forever: *Survey Monkey*. Is it possible to purchase any product or service, or make any kind of corporate inquiry, without immediately receiving an opportunity via email or phone to "Tell Us How We're Doing"? I'm all for letting someone know they've done a great job when service is exceptional. I tell people this whenever it's warranted. Or I show it symbolically, say in a restaurant, with a 20 percent tip. Conversely, if I'm disappointed about something, I'm not averse to sending a message or letter, or calling the subject business or party to complain. But, seriously, does every minor customer experience or interaction have to be rated? Can't there be a keypad code or box to check at the top of each survey page that says: "You're doing fine and, if not, I'll let you know." Is that too much to ask of the simian-fingered samplers? Now leave me alone.

The bark must taste good
Or the deer wouldn't chew it
Hidden in the trees

Home appliances have gotten too smart for their own good. No, make that for *our* own good. What happened to the days of plug it in, turn it on, and it works? Pretty soon we'll need a user I.D. and password just to dry our hair. I had to return a major brand smart TV because it didn't support my cable provider's app. My newly installed HVAC system has a digital thermostat that can't pick up Wi-Fi where it's located so I'm relegated to setting it manually instead of remotely via my cell phone from, say, a dinner party or while stuck in traffic. Are multiple functions dependent on the vagaries of a Bluetooth signal significantly better than performing one analog function well—you know, washing machines that wash and toasters that toast? Do I care if I'm able to defrost a chicken in the microwave with a verbal command? Can an Internet-enabled refrigerator make a reliable grocery list? But, as the techsters chide me, appliances are multi-taskers like people are supposed to be. They can do so much! Maybe that's why my sister-in-law covers the camera lens on her laptop and keeps "Siri" mute. Late at night in the living room "Alexa" cackles unbidden, your personal assistant device listening, anticipating every desire.

A flat of mushrooms
Propagating in the dark
Too many buttons

The super rich no longer crave *stuff*. After all, *anyone* can buy
a Rolex and a Land Rover Limousine, and it doesn't take long
to consume the exclusives from Bulgari, Cartier, Chopard.
And, honestly, how many bracelets from bespoke jewelers can
one wear on a yoga-toned arm without looking like a Times
Square hawker? What the super rich crave now are *experiences*
beyond the 8:00 PM dinner reservation at Nobu. How about
a reservation on the floor of the Colosseum (Rome, not L.A.)
for a fabulous first date; or luxury barge river cruises, all meals
prepared by dedicated Michelin-starred chefs; or jaunts via
the Four Seasons' corporate jet for a well-guarded weekend in
Rwanda; or residences on islands in archipelagos so remote
even their billionaire buddies haven't heard of them. Ooooo,
the bragging rights are *so delicious*! When I was in high school
we used to race our fathers' GM behemoths at the Rainbow
Beach parking lot in the emission shadow of Chicago's far south
side steel mills. Maybe when the global half-percenters get bored
with racing their bevies of Ferraris and Lamborghinis they'll
pick up a few '65 Electra 225s or '67 Delta 88s and try them
for experiential thrills. Because as it's been said, "The one thing
money can't buy is what money doesn't know exists."

Tree trimmers at work
Palm fronds are everywhere
You could thatch a hut

Unless you're wearing a kimono and your name is Toshiro, a "man bun" just doesn't work. And that goes double if it's paired with a lumberjack beard. I had my days of shoulder-length hair, Fu Manchu mustache, and oversized aviator glasses. I wore "rags and feathers from Salvation Army counters," once sent my mother screaming out of the house and into the street when I came home in a thrift store 1940s tuxedo jacket. After college, I had a pair of identical suits, probably bought together at a two-fer sale: one navy, one brown, wide double-breasted lapels, chalk stripes. I wore them to work on alternating days with equally cringe-worthy ties. I've survived bell bottoms, paisley polyester shirts with big dagger collars open to shark tooth pendants on thick gold chains. Been surrounded at parties by boomers sporting the record producer look, graying strands pulled back tight into ponytails. I've even lived long enough for ripped jeans to become *Easy Rider* cool again. But I thank God I was too early (or too late) for sagging, which gets my vote for the most perilous sartorial trend of all time—watching through my windshield as this kid duck-walks across Pico Boulevard against the light holding up XXL cargo pants at mid-thigh, baggy boxers billowing for all the world to see, as if in a desperate sack race trying not to get hit by a bus.

Sound of wind through pines
Waves keeping time in the dark
Some things refuse change

Truth to power. Truth will out. The truth shall set you free. We hold these truths to be self-evident. Some of my lies are true. True believer. Gospel truth. Half-truth. The truth, the whole truth, and nothing but the truth. Many a truth is spoken in jest. The truth is out there. Truth is stranger than fiction. *In vino veritas.* Beauty is truth, truth beauty. True north. True love. Grain of truth. True calling. My aim is true. Seek the truth. Speak the truth. Ring of truth. God's honest truth. True colors. Naked truth. Unvarnished truth. Truth, justice, and the American way. Moment of truth. Ain't it the truth?

Four in the morning
Play "Blues and the Abstract Truth"
Better than world news

A BRIEF AFTERWORD

The *haibun* form, three days of January rain, and the inevitable power outage thanks to Marina del Rey's third-world infrastructure. You'd think this condo block was in some Mumbai back alley with the world's craziest wire sculpture overhead, thousands of criss-crossing cables poaching the grid. I guess that's what happens when you landfill on old oil wells, subsoil prone to liquefaction when the overdue "big one" hits. It's 3:30 in the morning and I awaken still ruminating on the answer to a question posed during a radio interview on a show conducted almost entirely in Spanish, a language I barely speak and comprehend despite Miss Curtis' best efforts in high school. "Why do you write haibun?" the interviewer asked in halting English. With near-simultaneous Spanish translation provided by remarkable poet and writer Alicia Partnoy, I explained that I had come across the old Japanese form in poetry books by, first, Gary Snyder, and then Robert Hass and dismissed it, in my ignorance, as unpoetic, with those blocks of bulky prose and trailing short haiku-like poem attachments. Then I tried writing some and I saw what was machinating under the hood—the exposition then a dialogue with the reflective accompanying short poem that, if composed well, add layers of complexity, invite introspection, and hopefully (dare I say it?) offer some measure of enlightenment. The whole, again if written well, becomes a supercharged zen-like experience, a master's whack on the side of the head with a stick. "Ah," said the interviewer, "You fell in love." And, two haibun collections later, I guess I had. My decision, or compulsion, to write haibun was undergirded by my Westerner's fascination with all things Japanese, especially spirituality, consciousness, poetry, and art, along with reverence for nature. Any country that designates artists and craftspeople "Living National Treasures" has my vote. Specific to haibun, was my exposure to Sam Hamill's translation of *Narrow Road to the Interior*, Matsuo Bashō's travel journal written between 1690 and 1694, in which the form is shown to full narrative advantage. Then came additional dives: the centuries-old tradition of the Japanese literary or poetic diary; translations by Hass of haiku by Bashō, Buson, and Issa; a lovely four-volume seasonal compendium of haiku translated by R.H. Blyth; and Jane Hirshfield's superlative essay "Seeing Through Words: An Introduction to Bashō, Haiku, and the Suppleness of Image" in her book *Ten Windows*. But back to haibun love. Let me count the ways: I love the form's directness; its suppleness; its *plastique*-ness in all senses of the term, both flexible and explosive; as well as its tolerance of, and receptivity to, contemporary creative experimentation and variation. And now it's 5:21 a.m., my cat's awake, and it's time to address the issue that's become stickier of late than the insides of those little insect box traps I used to put down on my garage floor in Arizona, an issue that smells worse than hot roofing tar—cultural appropriation. As I wrote in my first haibun collection, *52 Views: The Haibun Variations*, published in 2013, the poems I craft are "written in the manner of haibun" and are "an interpretation of haibun form run through my coarse American filter" with the short commentary poems in the accepted American haiku rendition of three-line, 5-7-5 syllable structure. I'm obviously not Japanese and don't, and could never, have seventeenth century Japanese sensibilities. But that, to me, doesn't mean I can't or shouldn't attempt haibun, vary and integrate my version of the form into the roiling global poetry mix. Should I not attempt to write a Petrarchan sonnet because I'm not Italian? Or a Shakespearean sonnet because I'm not British? Or attempt to write a blues form when I'm not black from Mississippi? Or attempt the ghazal form when I'm not of Arabic ancestry? The ancient Romans adopted the Greek gods, hoovered up whatever culture they encountered, although which culture, adopter or adoptee, benefited most is debatable. Or, to throw a further change-up pitch here: supermarket sushi is ubiquitous these days, as are tacos and quesadillas. Should we not enjoy them because we're *gaijin* and *gringos* and not in Japan or Mexico? I don't know about you, but I don't think for a second I'm making authentic *pad thai*, or down-home collard greens, or baba ganoush in my kitchen. It's all adaptation and imagination. Imitation is the sincerest form of appreciation.

Pruning and pruning
Prose bush, seventeen branches
No perfect haibun

NOTES

Comet fears: The last line of the haiku was inspired by Nina Diamond.

My wife and I talk on Skype: The word "awesome" is awesomely overused. To see the word graphically defined, watch the western Greenland glacier calving scene in the documentary film *Chasing Ice:* https://www.youtube.com/watch?v=hC3VTgIPoGU

After Paris in December: The lyric quoted is from the song "California" by Joni Mitchell. In the second haiku's last line, "exquisite corpse" refers both to the dead bird and to the parlour game of the same name *(cadaver exquis)* credited to French surrealists Yves Tanguy, Marcel Duchamp, Jaques Prévert, and Andre Breton, in 1925. The game, according to the Tate Museum, entails players writing (or drawing) in turn on a sheet of paper, folding it to conceal what they have written or drawn, and then passing it on to the next player.

When this brutal winter: The last line of the haiku comes from the blues song "Drowning on Dry Land" by Roy Buchanan.

If patriotism is the last refuge: The haiku references the 1938 ballad "Prelude to a Kiss" composed by Duke Ellington, with lyrics by Irving Gordon and Irving Mills. Check out Sarah Vaughn's version on YouTube: https://www.youtube.com/watch?v=V34nkmFQfWM

The lyrics quoted in **My cat Dante** are from "The Ballad of Davy Crockett," the theme song of the Disney television series.

Another action film: The haiku refers to a quote attributed to French composer Claude Debussy (1862-1918): "Music is in the space between the notes."

Climate change naysayers: Record global heat becomes more alarming as it progresses—as will its consequences. According to research referenced in *The Guardian*, "Recent studies show the 20 warmest years on record have been in the past 22 years, and the top four in the past four years." *("David Attenborough: Collapse of Civilisation Is on the Horizon," 12/4/18)*

"Clocks" in the haiku is the term for dandelion puffballs.

There's a reason: As reported in *The Guardian* (January 20, 2019), the number of billionaires owning assets worth more than the wealth of the lowest half the world population has dropped from 80 when this haibun was originally written to 61 in 2016 to 43 in 2017 to the 26 cited in the 2018 Oxfam findings, delivered to correspond with the meeting of the World Economic Forum, the annual gathering of the rich and powerful at Davos, Switzerland.

The last line of prose in **It could be said** is taken from the 1931 song "Which Side Are You On?" written by Florence Reece, wife of a United Mine Workers Union organizer in Harlan County, Kentucky. It was later popularized by folk singer Pete Seeger.

Safe, Warm, If, L.A.: The title and haiku feature lyrics from songs of the time and place: "I'd be safe and warm if I was in L.A." from "California Dreamin" by The Mommas and the Poppas; "No one here gets out alive" from "Five to One" by The Doors; "Fountain of Sorrow" by Jackson Browne; "This old world keep spinnin' round" from "Comes a Time" by Neil Young; " You can check out any time you like, but you can never leave" from "Hotel California" by The Eagles; and "I felt unfettered and alive" from "Free Man in Paris" by Joni Mitchell.

With great admiration and respect, **I hear about the steel mill** borrows lines from iconic poems by two of America's finest poets: "What Work Is" by Philip Levine and "Degrees of Gray in Philipsburg" by Richard Hugo.

The actress explains was inspired by K.N.

I blame it on the aliens: My apologies—I've been watching way too many episodes and seasons of *Ancient Aliens*. The Verna reference comes from Jack Finney's short story "Of Missing Persons" that I read in my grammar school reader and have never forgotten. The same is true of the original 1951 version of *The Day the Earth Stood Still*, with Michael Rennie and Patricia Neal. "Gort! Klaatu barrada nikto."

I'm taking up chess: While writing this haibun I kept thinking of the Chris Rea lyric in his song "The Road to Hell"—"This ain't no technological breakdown. / Oh no, this is the road to hell."

In the aborted experiment mentioned, Facebook "chatbots" independently developed their own language incomprehensible to humans. Check this *Forbes* link for the full story: https://www.forbes.com/sites/tonybradley/2017/07/31/facebook-ai-creates-its-own-language-in-creepy-preview-of-our-potential-future/#6fe5ee4d292c.

In another disturbing AI-related story, Amazon Echo smart speakers (anthropomorphised as virtual assistant Alexa) began laughing spontaneously. Here's a link to the NPR story: https://www.npr.org/sections/thetwo-way/2018/03/08/591831871/alexa-please-stop-laughing-amazon-says-its-fixing-device-s-unprompted-cackles

Just because mentions yet another group of ongoing dystopian fields of "inquiry." As humorist Dave Barry says, "I am not making this up."

Beyond belief is in memory of John Wiebusch.

El Al just lost a court case: The lyric that forms the last line of the haiku is from the Cole Porter song "Anything Goes": "In olden days, a glimpse of stocking / Was looked on as something shocking. / But now, God knows, / Anything goes."

Istanbul uses a number of Turkish and Arabic words: *simit* are bagel-like round breads sold at stalls all over Istanbul; *dondurma* is the signature wonderfully gooey form of Turkish ice cream; *abayat, niquab,* and *hijab* refer to types of women's head coverings; *madrassas* are religious schools, some of which are associated with radicalizing Muslim youth; *sheesha* is the term for hookah waterpipes and also the variety of tobacco smoked in them.

The "roofalanche" in **Fire and water** refers to sometimes deadly snowslides from slanted roofs that can occure after heavy snowfalls.

The swamp referred to in **An overflowing swamp** is the metaphorical one in Washington D.C. filled with lobbyists and corruption, alligators and snakes. Donald Trump promised he would "drain" it during his 2016 presidential election campaign; instead he dredged it deeper. I couldn't help recalling the prophetic quote from French writer Voltaire (1694-1778): *"Tyrants have always some slight shade of virtue; they support the laws before destroying them."*

The literary world ends with a lyric by Bob Dylan from his song "The Times They Are A-Changin'."

The reference in **Back when I was a kid** is to HUAC, the House Un-American Activities Committee that, according to the Eleanor Roosevelt Papers Project, "was created in 1938 to investigate alleged disloyalty and subversive activities on the part of private citizens, public employees, and those organizations suspected of having Communist ties…the questioning style and examination techniques employed by HUAC served as the model upon which Senator Joseph McCarthy would conduct his investigative hearings in the early 1950s."

The super rich was sparked by the article "The Experience Wars" by Horacio Silva in the October 2018 issue of *Town & Country*.

"Blues and the Abstract Truth" referenced in the haiku for **Truth to power** is a cut on the classic jazz album of the same name by Oliver Nelson.

ACKNOWLEDGMENTS

Thanks to these print and online journals and anthologies where the following haibun, sometimes in slightly different form, have previously appeared:

Cultural Weekly: "Westbound on Interstate 10"

Hayden's Ferry Review: "After Paris in December" and "Hoarder Alert"

The Los Angeles Review: "Climate Change Naysayers" and "I've Lived Long Enough"

Serving House Journal: "How Fitting"

Spillway: "If Patriotism Is the Last Refuge"

"Safe, Warm, If, L.A." appears in the anthology *L.A. in the 1970s: Weird Scenes Inside the Gold Mine*

"Researchers Report" appears in the *San Diego Poetry Annual 2014-15*

"Westbound on Interstate 10" appears in the anthology *Los Angeles Water Works*

My unending gratitude to the following for their encouragement, support, and editorial expertise:

David St. John, Susan Terris, Marvin Bell, Jane Hirshfield, Richard Garcia, Chris Merrill, Dorothy Barresi, Mifanwy Kaiser, Dante, and the poets of the Venice Collective: Marjorie Becker, Jeanette Clough, Dina Hardy, Paul Lieber, Holaday Mason, Sarah Maclay, Jan Wesley, Brenda Yates, and Mariano Zaro.

TEBOT BACH
A 501 (c) (3) Literary Arts Education Non Profit

THE TEBOT BACH MISSION: advancing literacy, strengthening community, and transforming life experiences with the power of poetry through readings, workshops, and publications.

THE TEBOT BACH PROGRAMS
1. A poetry reading and writing workshop series for venues such as homeless shelters, battered women's shelters, nursing homes, senior citizen daycare centers, Veterans organizations, hospitals, AIDS hospices, correctional facilities which serve under-represented populations. Participating poets include: John Balaban, Brendan Constantine, Megan Doherty, Richard Jones, Dorianne Laux, M.L. Leibler, Laurence Lieberman, Carol Moldaw, Patricia Smith, Arthur Sze, Carine Topal, Cecilia Woloch.

2. A poetry reading and writing workshop series for the Southern California community at large, and for schools K-University. The workshops have featured local, national, and international teaching poets; David St. John, Charles Webb, Wanda Coleman, Amy Gerstler, Patricia Smith, Holly Prado, Dorothy Lux, Rebecca Seiferle, Suzanne Lummis, Michael Datcher, B.H. Fairchild, Cecilia Woloch, Chris Abani, Laurel Ann Bogen, Sam Hamill, David Lehman, Christopher Buckley, and Mark Doty.

3. A publishing component to give local, national, and international poets a venue for publishing and distribution.

Tebot Bach
Box 7887
Huntington Beach, CA 92615-7887
714-968-0905
www.tebotbach.org